Hop To It!

Appliquéd Blocks & Projects

By *Edyta Sitar* for *Laundry Basket Quilts*

Landauer Publishing

Acknowledgements

A very special "Thank You" is extended to the many skilled hands and patient minds that have helped me to make this book possible:

- My loving family and friends who support me in everything I do

- Moda Fabrics for the opportunity to design beautiful fabrics that are the starting point for my quilts

- Julie Lillo and Pam Henrys for adding the special touch to the machine quilting in these projects

- Scott and Curtis for welcoming me to their home and gardens where photography was taken

- Dennis and Sue who were able to capture the beautiful colors with their camera lenses

- The Landauer Publishing team for their patience, expertise and seemingly endless hours in bringing this book to life

- All the quilters who have enjoyed my designs over the years

This book was designed, produced, and published by Landauer Corporation
3100 NW 101st Street, Urbandale, IA 50322
800-557-2144; www.landauercorp.com

President/Publisher: Jeramy Lanigan Landauer
Vice President of Sales & Operations: Kitty Jacobson
Managing Editor: Jeri Simon
Art Director: Lyne Neymeyer
Technical Illustrator: Janet Pittman
Technical Editors: Heidi Kaisand and Rhonda Matus
Photography: Dennis Craft—Craft Photographic Gallery
   and Sue Voegtlin

Library of Congress Control Number: 2008937243

ISBN 13: 978-0-9818040-1-9
ISBN 10: 0-9818040-1-2

This book is printed on acid-free paper.
Printed in U.S.A.
10 9 8 7 6 5 4 3 2

Contents

Foreword
From the Author...

"Do you remember the joy you experienced as a child when you received a new coloring book and crayons? To me, appliquéing is like coloring with fabrics and I hope you agree after enjoying the projects in this wonderful book.

Through this book, I want to take you back in time to the amazing feeling you experienced as you covered the empty spaces with stunning colors. Black and white images of wreaths, flowers, and simple silhouettes of nature allow you to pour gorgeous colors and add little details to make the designs all your own. The variety of projects and techniques will allow you to gather experience and have a great time. No matter which quilt or project you choose you will gain new skills and knowledge. Don't hesitate; hop to it! Fill your soul and your hands with joyful color."

Edyta Sitar

Starting with Color

To help you create a beautiful quilt project, I want to share with you the techniques I've developed for selecting colors and fabrics. These techniques will help you achieve pleasing results and add to your joy of quilting.

Finding Inspiration

For inspiration when designing my quilts and selecting a color palette, I look carefully to my garden and nature to see the myriad of colors and nature's sense of order, balance, and beauty. For example, not all leaves in nature are green. Some may be blue, rust, gray, or burgundy. Notice in your own surroundings how light, shade, time of year, or angle of the sun during the day affects and changes the color. Basing your selections on what you truly see and observe rather than relying on what you hold in your mind will open up many expressive possibilities for you.

Preparing to Select Colors and Fabrics

To begin the color and fabric selection process I first look at a black and white drawing of the block design. I see the types and sizes of the shapes I'll be picking fabric and colors for, as well as the flowers, leaves, animals, or other subjects.

I choose from my entire fabric stash and set a large plastic baby pool in the room as a container to hold the fabrics as I select them. A clean table top will work just as well.

Selecting the Colors and Fabrics

My quilts combine both batik fabrics and fabrics with traditional patterns. To ensure I have a good balance of colors and patterns throughout the quilt, I've developed a selection process I call "The Rule of Five."

To demonstrate, we'll go through the color and fabric palette selected for the featured quilt *From My Garden Album Quilt*. **Note:** The *Dreaming In Color* batik fabric line I designed for Moda is the base for many of the projects in this book. There are three main steps:

- **Selecting the color palette**
- **Selecting the fabrics within each color using the Rule of Five**
- **Assembling a combination of colors and fabrics into a "Kit" for each block**

From my entire fabric stash I select a favorite for each color—a favorite green, blue, red, mustard, and so on.
Then, to ensure I have a variety of pattern sizes and colors I apply the Rule of Five.

The Rule of Five always includes:
1. A Small Scale Print
2. A Medium Scale Print
3. A Large Scale Print
4. A Stripe
5. A Polka Dot

Using blue as an example, I select my favorite blue as the middle of the color range. Then I'll select four to five blue fabrics lighter than the favorite and four to five fabrics darker than the favorite. Here's where the Rule of Five comes in. Within this range of approximately ten fabrics, I'll choose patterns that fit into the Rule of Five categories. Not all of the fabrics in the resulting group of ten will have a pattern, but at least five of them should follow the Rule of Five.

> **Note:** *Use the colors and fabric at right and on the following pages as your guide in making your own color and fabric selections for the From My Garden Album Quilt and the other projects. The favorite color fabric is designated with a dot.*

Here's the favorite

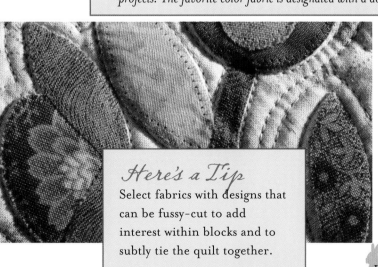

Here's a Tip
Select fabrics with designs that can be fussy-cut to add interest within blocks and to subtly tie the quilt together.

The Rule of Five

1. Small scale print
Small scale prints appear as an overall texture when viewed from a distance.

2. Medium scale print
Traditional prints often fall into the medium scale print catagory

3. Large scale print
My batik fabric designs offer a variety of colors and print sizes.

4. Stripe
Stripes aren't always straight lines. Look for prints with line elements.

5. Polka Dot
Fabric patterns with designs that create spots of color will look like dots when viewed from a distance.

Fabric &
Color Guide

Blues

Blue-greens

Greens

Golds

Fabric &
Color Guide

Rusts

Purples

Background
Fabric & Color
Guide

Browns

Neutrals

Selecting a Block Kit

The next stage in the selection process is to create the fabric "Kits" for use in one or more of the blocks in the quilt. With the separate color stacks in front of me, I pull fabrics from each color stack to form a new multi-color stack or "Kit" of fabrics containing eight to ten selections. I use my block layout as my guide to remind myself of the images—leaves, branches, berries, and so on—I would like to cover with fabric. Each multi-color stack follows the Rule of Five and contains at least one of each print type. I will use some of the fabrics in more than one block to ensure the finished blocks will be cohesive in color when the quilt is assembled.

The Rule of Five also applies to the background fabric for your blocks. Choose your background color palette. Select a favorite shade within the color you have chosen for your background. Select lighter and darker fabrics within that color until you have a total of 10. Follow the Rule of Five and have at least one of each fabric pattern.

Here's a Tip

Use a digital camera to take a photo of your Fabric Kits to get a feel for the color and value combinations in your block. Over time you will become more comfortable using the Rule of Five. Having the fabrics in a container helps you stay focused on the selected fabrics.

Techniques

In this section you'll find clear step-by-step photos and how-to instructions for fusible, machine, and hand appliqué techniques. Choose your favorite method and hop to it!

Fusible Appliqué

This style of appliqué has become my personal favorite. With a little patience and the right materials you can achieve excellent results in a short period of time. I also find it to be a relaxing and enjoyable technique.

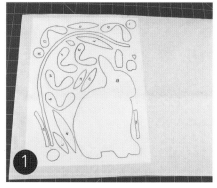

Supplies
—Light fusible webbing, pressing sheet, sharp scissors, traced block layout, reversed appliqué pieces, pencil, cotton thread, invisible thread, embroidery needle for machine, background fabric, and desired appliqué fabric

Note: All shapes are conveniently reversed for this technique.

To prepare the appliqués, place the fusible webbing, paper side up on the reversed appliqué shapes. Trace each appliqué shape, including any dashed lines, onto the fusible webbing. Mark each shape with its corresponding letter to help you place the pieces correctly on the layout.

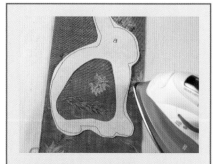

Cut out the appliqué shapes from the fusible webbing leaving at least ¹/₈" of fusible webbing around the outside of each shape. You may cut the fusible webbing from the center of the larger pieces, if you wish.

Here's a Tip
To remove the fusible webbing from the center of larger template shapes, such as the bunny, cut into the center of the webbing with a sharp scissors. Cut out the center leaving approximately ¹/₄" inside the traced line.

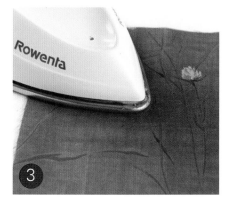

Press your fabrics before fusing to be sure there are no wrinkles or creases.

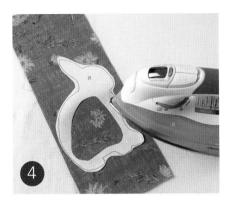

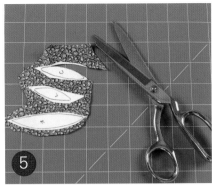

Fuse each appliqué shape by pressing it to the wrong side of the desired color fabric following manufacturer's directions. Use the picture as a color guide or use a color suggested in the block instructions. **Note:** Do not overheat fusible webbing.

Cut the appliqué shapes out EXACTLY on the traced line. Achieve nice smooth edges by using the back blades of a sharp scissors and making long cuts.

Place the traced layout guide under the pressing sheet on an ironing board. Proceed to prepare the appliqué pieces to place on the background.

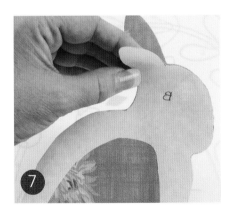

Peel the fusible webbing paper from each shape.
Note: If you crease the edge of the paper it will peel off easier.

After all the paper is peeled off, place each fabric appliquéd shape on top of the pressing sheet, following the layout underneath as a placement guide.
Note: Remember the dashed lines indicate where the fabric shapes overlap each other.

Press the appliqué shapes together *only* where the fabric appliqués overlap. Press gently to secure these pieces together. Make sure all your pieces stay on the layout and use it as your guide.

Fusible Appliqué

To prepare the background fabric for cutting, press it to remove any wrinkles or creases.

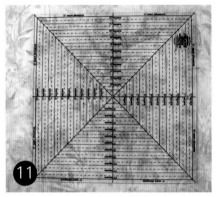

Each block will require a 12" square of background fabric.

Here's a Tip
Cut the background fabric for each block $\frac{1}{2}$" larger than what the instructions call for. This extra $\frac{1}{2}$" allows you to square up your block after it is completed.

Peel the group of appliqué shapes from the pressing sheet and place in the center of the background fabric square block. Press in place.

Here's a Tip
To lock your stitches when sewing, overlap the beginning and ending stitches. Gently pull all the thread to the back once the block is completed.

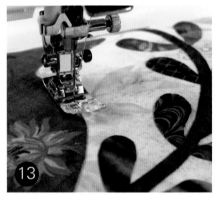

Prepare your sewing machine for appliquéing by using invisible nylon thread in the top and cotton thread to match the background fabric in the bobbin. Set your machine to sew a small $\frac{1}{8}$" zigzag stitch.
Position the needle on the edge of an appliqué shape. Stitch around all edges of the appliqués keeping the zigzag very small. Most of the stitch should be over the appliqué piece and only one needle width on the background next to the edge of your appliqué.

Stitch Style
Zigzag around the edge of the appliqué with only 1 needle width onto block background.

Here's a Tip
Before beginning to stitch my appliqués, I set my sewing machine's top tension at one (1), stitch width one (1), and stitch length one-and-a-half (1$\frac{1}{2}$).
Test your machine's settings on a piece of scrap fabric before you begin stitching the appliqués to the background fabric. Make any adjustments needed to achieve the correct size zigzag stitch.
If your machine is bringing the bobbin thread to the top of your appliqué, you may need to lower the top tension.

When you have completed stitching the shapes to the background block, gently press the finished block from the back. This will heal any holes left by the needle. Be careful that the iron is not too hot.

Trim the block to 12" square. This includes the $\frac{1}{4}$" seam allowance needed when sewing it to the quilt top.

Machine Appliqué

For a technique that mimics the look of hand appliqué, but is much quicker to complete, try machine appliqué. You will have beautiful projects finished in no time.

Supplies—Traced block layout, freezer paper, scissors, desired appliqué fabric, cotton thread, nylon thread, quilting needle for your machine, background fabric, and water soluble glue stick

Note: For machine appliqué you will be using the traced block layout to trace and place the appliqué shapes, NOT reversed appliqué pieces.

Here's a Tip

Always use a complete layout of the appliqué block, including the dashed lines and any other markings. Refer to this layout as a guide for arranging the appliqué pieces. Remember: dashed lines indicate where appliqué shapes overlap each other.

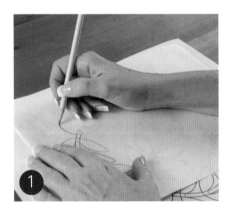

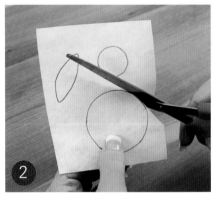

Carefully trace all the appliquéd shapes for your block from the layout to the matte side of the freezer paper. Be sure to trace the dashed lines. These lines indicate where the appliqués will overlap.

Cut out all the freezer paper templates exactly on the traced lines. A smooth even cut will ensure even edges and lovely appliqués.
Note: When cutting out the paper templates use the back part of the scissor blades. This will give you a smooth even edge.

Add a touch of water soluble glue to the matte side of the freezer paper pattern and finger-press it to the wrong side of your chosen fabric.

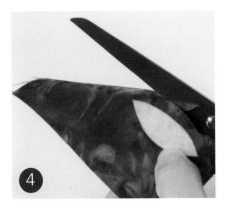

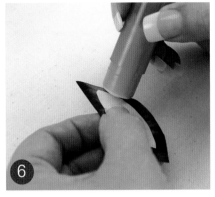

Carefully cut the fabric ¼" away from the shape's outside edge. The ¼" of fabric will be turned over the template.

Clip in ³⁄₁₆" on all edges leaving ½" between cuts. This will allow the fabric to be turned effortlessly. Do not cut too close to the freezer paper pattern.

Use glue as needed to assist in turning the edges of the appliqués over the freezer paper, especially the tips.

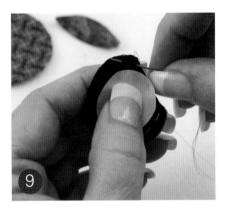

Use the tip of an iron on a cotton dry setting to turn the ¼" of fabric over the freezer paper template. Hold for a few seconds to allow the fabric to adhere to the shiny side of the freezer paper.

Continue until all edges of the appliqués are turned. Add an extra dab of glue if needed.

To turn a circle shape use a basting stitch around the ¼" seam allowance of the appliqué piece.

Once your appliqué pieces are prepared it is time to assemble the block.

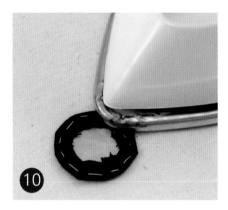

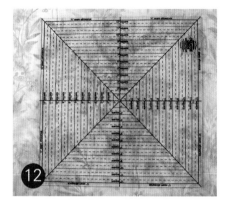

Pull the stitches together and press the seam allowances to the shiny side of freezer paper.

To prepare the background fabric for cutting, press it to remove any wrinkles or creases.

Each block will require a 12" square of background fabric.

Here's a Tip

Cut the background fabric for each block ½" larger than what the instructions call for. This extra ½" allows you to square up your block after it is completed.

Stitch Style

Zigzag around the edge of the appliqué piece with only 1 needle width on the appliqué.

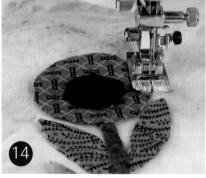

Press and lightly starch the background fabric. Referring to the traced block layout, place the appliqué shapes on the background fabric. Press the shapes in place. The shiny side of the freezer paper will hold the appliqué pieces in place. If necessary, use a touch of water soluble glue.

To prepare your sewing machine for stitching use nylon invisible thread in the top and cotton thread to match the background fabric in the bobbin. Set your machine to sew a very small zigzag stitch, 20 stitches to an inch.

While stitching be sure half the zigzag is showing on the appliqué shape and half on the background fabric.

Here's a Tip

Before beginning to stitch my appliqués, I set my sewing machine's tension at one (1), stitch width one (1), and stitch length one (1).

Test your machine's settings on a piece of scrap fabric before you begin stitching the appliqués to the background fabric. Make any adjustments needed to achieve the correct size zigzag stitch.

If your machine is bringing the bobbin thread to the top of your appliqué, you may need to lower the top tension.

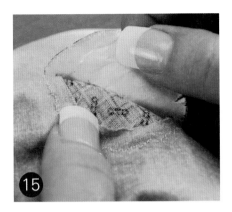

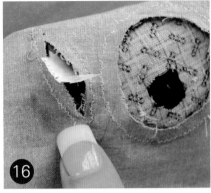

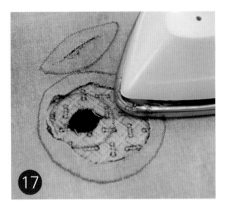

Once the appliqués have been stitched to the background fabric, the freezer paper must be removed. Turn your block to the back. With a very sharp scissors make a gentle cut in the background fabric under the appliqué pieces and carefully remove the freezer paper.

Continue until all freezer paper appliqués have been removed.

After appliqué is complete press the block from the back to avoid 'shining' the edges of your appliquéd pieces. Square your block to exactly 12" in preparation for setting it in the quilt.

Hand Appliqué

When hand appliquéing I prefer the starch method. Once all the pieces are prepared, hand appliqué is a wonderfully relaxing stitching technique.

Supplies—Freezer paper, starch, desired appliqué fabric, silk thread, appliqué needle, traced block layout, scissors, background fabric square, and water soluble glue stick (optional)

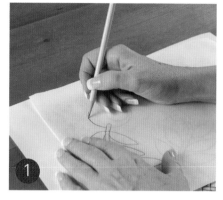

Note: For hand appliqué you will be using the full block layout to trace and place the appliqué shapes, NOT reversed appliqué pieces.

To create paper templates, carefully trace all appliquéd shapes from the layout to the matte side of the freezer paper. Mark the letters from the patterns onto the templates. Be sure to trace the dashed lines. These lines indicate where the appliqués will overlap.

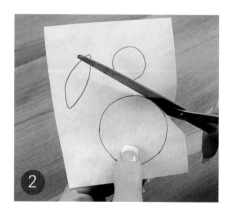

Cut out all the freezer paper templates exactly on the traced lines. A smooth cut will insure even and lovely appliqués.

Here's a Tip

When cutting out the paper templates use the blades closest to the handles of the scissors. This will give you smooth and even edges.

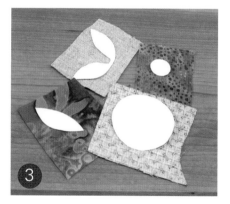

Add a touch of water soluble glue to the matte side of the freezer paper pattern and finger-press it to the wrong side of your chosen fabric.

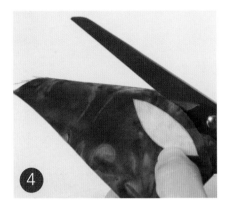

Carefully cut the fabric ¼" away from the shape's outside edge. The ¼" of fabric will be turned over the template.

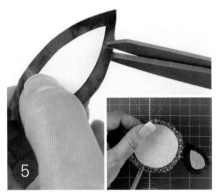

Clip in ³⁄₁₆" on all edges leaving ½" between cuts. This will allow the fabric to be turned effortlessly. Do not cut too close to the edge of the freezer paper template.

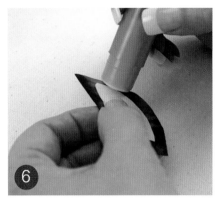

Use glue as needed to assist in turning the edges of the appliqués over the freezer paper.

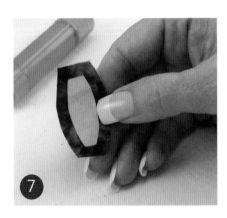

Use your fingertips to turn the tips or difficult edges of the appliqué toward the shiny side of the freezer paper.

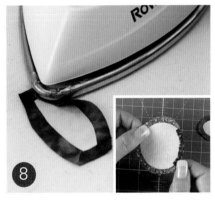

Use the tip of an iron on a cotton dry setting to turn the ¼" of fabric over the freezer paper template. Hold for a few seconds to allow the fabric to adhere to the shiny side of the freezer paper.

You may also lightly spritz spray starch or run the water soluble glue stick on the ¼" of fabric outside the traced line and use your fingertips to turn the fabric edges toward the freezer paper.

To turn a circle shape use a basting stitch around the ¼" seam allowance of the appliqué piece.

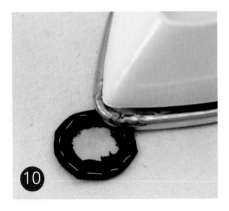

10 Pull the stitches together and press the seam allowances to the shiny side of freezer paper.

11 Continue until all edges of the appliqués are turned. Add an extra dab of glue if needed.

12 To prepare the background fabric for cutting, press it to remove any wrinkles or creases.

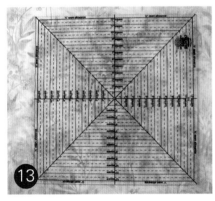

13 Each block requires a 12" square of background fabric.

Here's a Tip
You may wish to cut the background fabric for each block ½" larger than what the instructions call for. This extra ½" allows you to square up your block after it is completed.

14 Refer to the traced full block pattern to lay out the appliqué shapes on the background fabric. Press the shapes in place. If necessary, use a dab of water soluble glue or spray starch to hold the shapes in place.

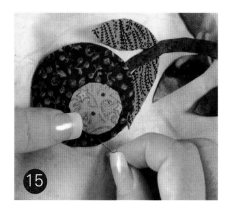

Appliqué the fabric shapes to the background fabric using silk thread and an appliqué needle. Sew a small slipstitch around the edges of all the pieces.

Once the appliqués have been stitched to the background fabric, the freezer paper must be removed. Turn your block to the back. With a very sharp scissors make a gentle cut in the background fabric under the appliqué pieces and carefully remove the freezer paper. Continue until all freezer paper appliqués have been removed.

Always press the block from the back to avoid 'shining' the edges of your appliquéd pieces.

Square your block to exactly 12" in preparation for setting it in the quilt.

From My Garden Album Quilt

Experience the joy of bringing to life a quilted work of art as you fill the silhouetted designs in this 12-block Album Quilt with glorious splashes of color

Materials

- 12—18" x 22" pieces (fat quarters) of assorted off-white prints for appliqué foundations and sashing
- 1 yard of multi-color batik for sashing squares and inner border
- 1½ yards of dark green batik for outer border
- ¾ yard of light green batik for binding
- 10—⅛ yard pieces of assorted warm color (yellow, orange, red, rust, purple) prints and batiks for sashing
- 5—18" x 22" pieces (fat quarters) of assorted brown prints for appliqués
- 6—⅛ yard pieces of assorted red prints and batiks for appliqués
- 6—⅛ yard pieces of assorted blue prints and batiks for appliqués
- 6—⅛ yard pieces of assorted gold prints and batiks for appliqués
- 10—18" x 22" pieces (fat quarters) of assorted green prints and batiks for appliqués
- 2" square of solid black
- 4 yards of backing fabric
- 70" x 84" of quilt batting

Finished appliqué blocks: 11½" square
Finished quilt: 63½" x 77⅞"
Measurements include ¼" seam allowances

Cut the Fabrics

From assorted off-white prints, cut:

12—12" inch square appliqué foundations

62—$4^{1/8}$" squares, cutting each diagonally in an X for a total of 248 sashing triangles

2—$3^{3/4}$" squares, cutting each in half diagonally for a total of 4 corner sashing triangles

From multi-color batik, cut:

7—$3^{3/8}$ x 44" strips for inner border

16—$3^{3/8}$" squares for sashing squares

From green batik, cut:

8—$6^{3/8}$" x 44" strips for outer border

From light green batik, cut:

8—$2^{1/2}$" x 44" strips for binding

From assorted warm color (yellow, orange, red, rust, purple) prints and batiks, cut:

62—$4^{1/8}$" squares, cutting each diagonally in an X for a total of 248 sashing triangles

2—$3^{3/4}$" squares, cutting each in half diagonally for a total of 4 corner sashing triangles

Cut and Assemble the Appliqué Blocks

The instructions that follow are for cutting out each of the 12 blocks in *My Garden Album Quilt*. The blocks are named, as well as labeled 1 through 12, with the pieces in each block labeled A-Z. Use the appliqué method of your choice on pages 18-31 to prepare the appliqué pieces.

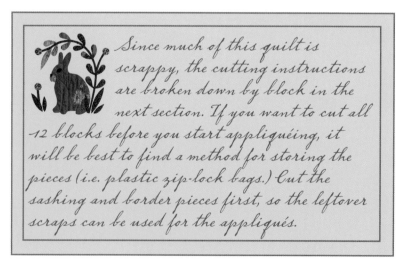

Since much of this quilt is scrappy, the cutting instructions are broken down by block in the next section. If you want to cut all 12 blocks before you start appliquéing, it will be best to find a method for storing the pieces (i.e. plastic zip-lock bags.) Cut the sashing and border pieces first, so the leftover scraps can be used for the appliqués.

From My Garden Album Quilt

Designed and pieced by Edyta Sitar; machine quilted by Julie Lillo

Block 1 – Rose Hip Heart

WHEN YOU LOOK CLOSELY YOU CAN SEE HOW THIS HEART-SHAPED
DESIGN DISPLAYS NATURE'S GREENS IN A BEAUTIFUL ARRAY OF
COLORS AND PATTERNS TO GIVE THE BLOCK BEAUTY AND VARIETY.

Note: Diagram not to scale; for color placement only.

Block 1–Rose Hip Heart Cutting Instructions

From brown prints, cut:
1 *each* of patterns A, B, E, F, S, and T
2 *each* of patterns C and D

From red prints, cut:
6 of pattern H
1 of pattern P
2 of pattern R

From purple prints, cut:
2 of pattern K

From gold prints, cut:
6 of pattern I

From green prints, cut:
4 of pattern J
3 *each* of patterns L and M
1 *each* of patterns G, N, O, Q, U, and V

From My Garden Album Quilt
Block I - Rose Hip Heart

I square equals I inch

For machine and hand appliqué enlarge the block layout
and trace shapes exactly. Do not reverse.

Enlarge 150%

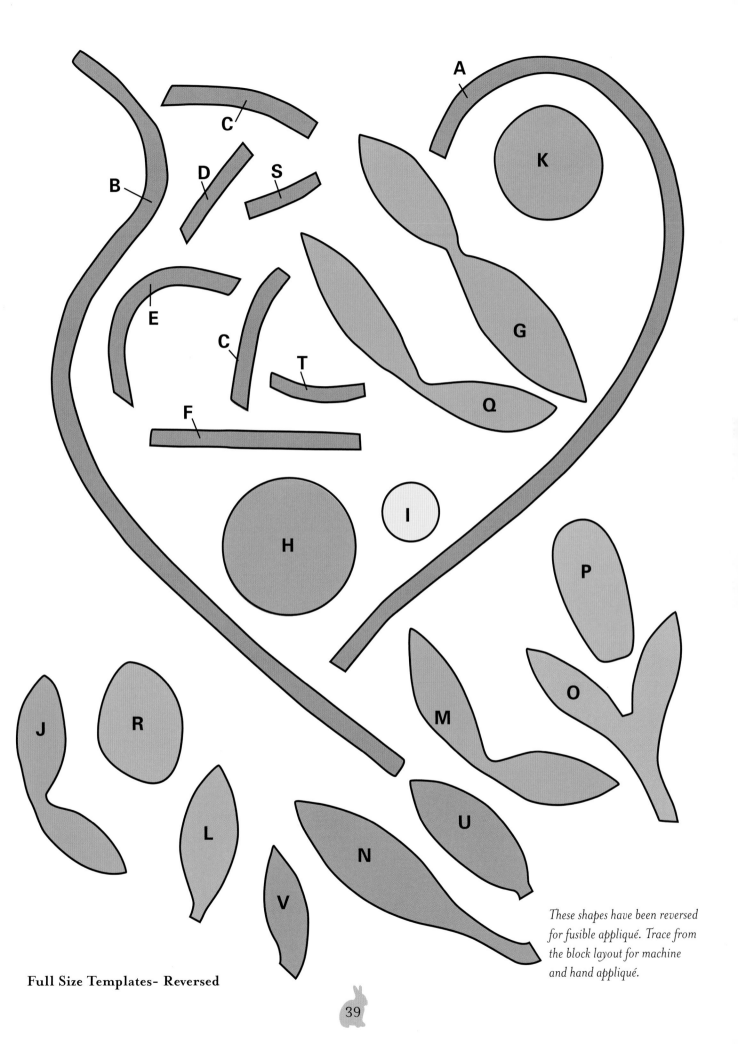

Full Size Templates- Reversed

These shapes have been reversed for fusible appliqué. Trace from the block layout for machine and hand appliqué.

Block 2 - Fleur Delight

Fluid stripes anchor buds and branches in an elegantly simple setting. A little fussy-cutting adds a bright blossom to the stem.

Note: Diagram not to scale; for color placement only.

Block 2-Fleur Delight
Cutting Instructions

From brown prints, cut:
1 *each* of patterns A, B, and C
3 of pattern E

From red prints, cut:
3 of pattern K

From blue prints, cut:
3 of pattern H

From green prints, cut:
1 *each* of patterns F, G, M, and D
3 of pattern I
2 *each* of patterns J and L

From My Garden Album Quilt
Block 2 - Fleur Delight

I square equals I inch

For machine and hand appliqué enlarge the block layout and trace shapes exactly. Do not reverse.

Enlarge 150%

A

B

D

E

C

F

M

L

J

G

K

H

I

These shapes have been reversed for fusible appliqué. Trace from the block layout for machine and hand appliqué.

Full Size Templates- Reversed

Block 3 – Rose of Sharon Wreath

THE ROSE OF SHARON TAKES CENTER STAGE BALANCED BY ROSE HIPS AND FOLIAGE IN REPEAT FABRICS AND COLORS.

Note: Diagram not to scale; for color placement only.

Block 3–Rose of Sharon Wreath
Cutting Instructions

From brown prints, cut:

4 of pattern A

1 *each* of patterns I and N

From green prints, cut:

4 *each* of patterns B and C

From red prints, cut:

3 of pattern E

1 *each* of patterns G and O

1 of pattern H

1 of pattern M

From gold prints, cut:

3 of pattern F

From blue prints, cut:

4 of pattern D

1 *each* of patterns J, K, and L

1 square equals 1 inch

For machine and hand appliqué enlarge the block layout
and trace shapes exactly. Do not reverse.

Enlarge 150%

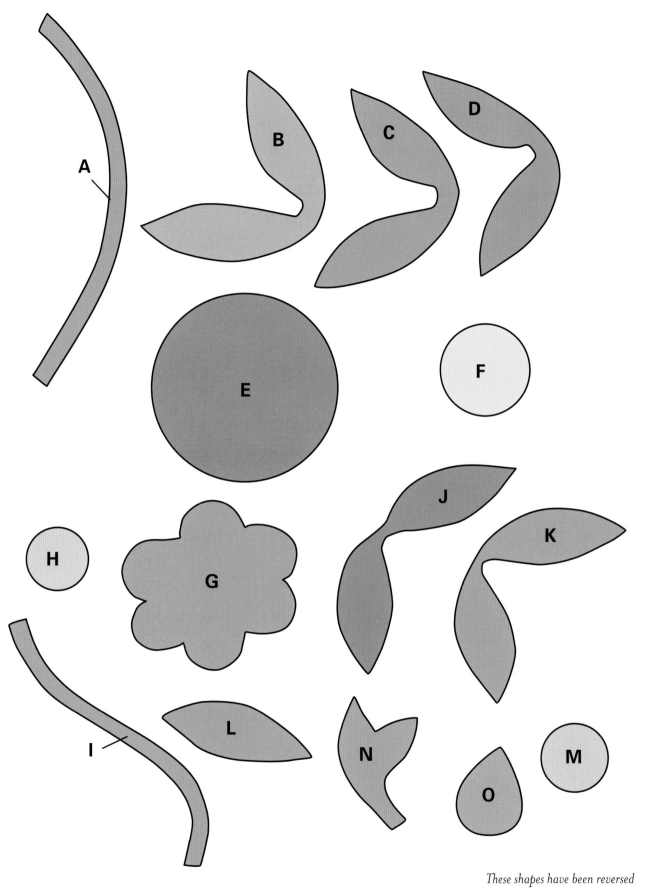

Full Size Templates- Reversed

These shapes have been reversed for fusible appliqué. Trace from the block layout for machine and hand appliqué.

Block 4 - Spring Reel

THE RESTFUL HUES OF BLUE FLOWERS ARE IRIDESCENT AGAINST
A SUBTLE YET SURPRISINGLY MULTI-COLORED BLOCK
BACKGROUND.

Note: Diagram not to scale; for color placement only.

Block 4-Spring Reel
Cutting Instructions

From blue prints, cut:

4 *each* of patterns E, F, and G

From gold prints, cut:

1 of pattern B

From green prints, cut:

1 of pattern A

4 *each* of patterns C and D

From My Garden Album Quilt
Block 4 - Spring Reel

1 square equals 1 inch

For machine and hand appliqué enlarge the block layout and trace shapes exactly. Do not reverse.

Enlarge 150%

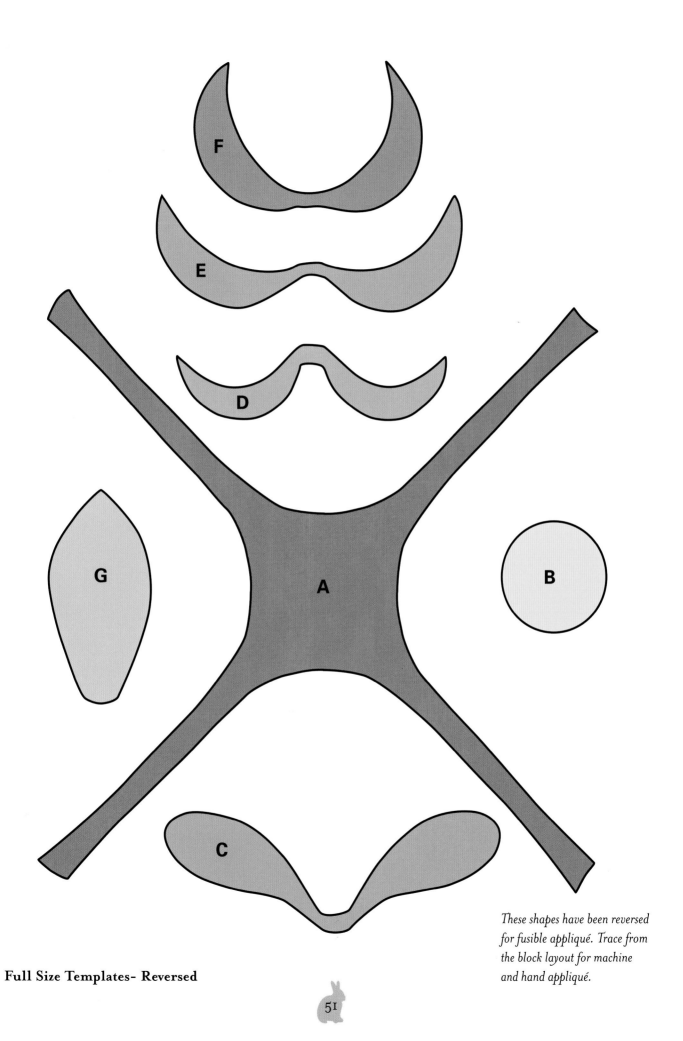

F

E

D

G

A

B

C

These shapes have been reversed for fusible appliqué. Trace from the block layout for machine and hand appliqué.

Full Size Templates- Reversed

Block 5 - Garden Guest

Fussy-cutting fabric brings life to buds and interest to a bunny visiting the garden in spring. The stripes, patterns, and dots in the leaves create visual harmony.

Note: Diagram not to scale; for color placement only.

Block 5-Garden Guest Cutting Instructions

From brown prints, cut:
1 *each* of patterns D, E, F, and G

From gray prints, cut:
1 *each* of patterns A and O

From red prints, cut:
1 *each* of patterns H, I, J, K, and P
3 of pattern N

From gold prints, cut:
1 of pattern M
1 of pattern L

From green prints, cut:
1 *each* of patterns L, R, and S
2 of pattern Q

From solid black, cut:
1 *each* of patterns B and C

53

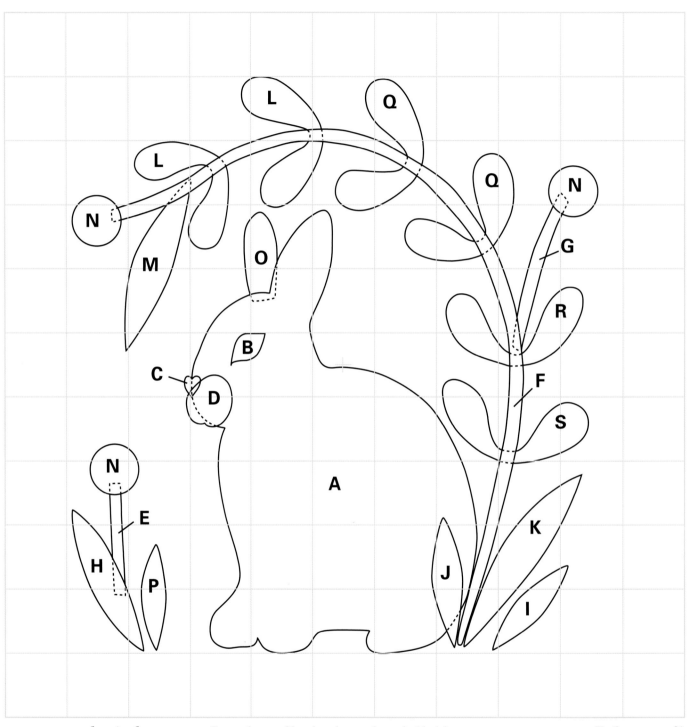

1 square equals 1 inch

For machine and hand appliqué enlarge the block layout and trace shapes exactly. Do not reverse.

Enlarge 150%

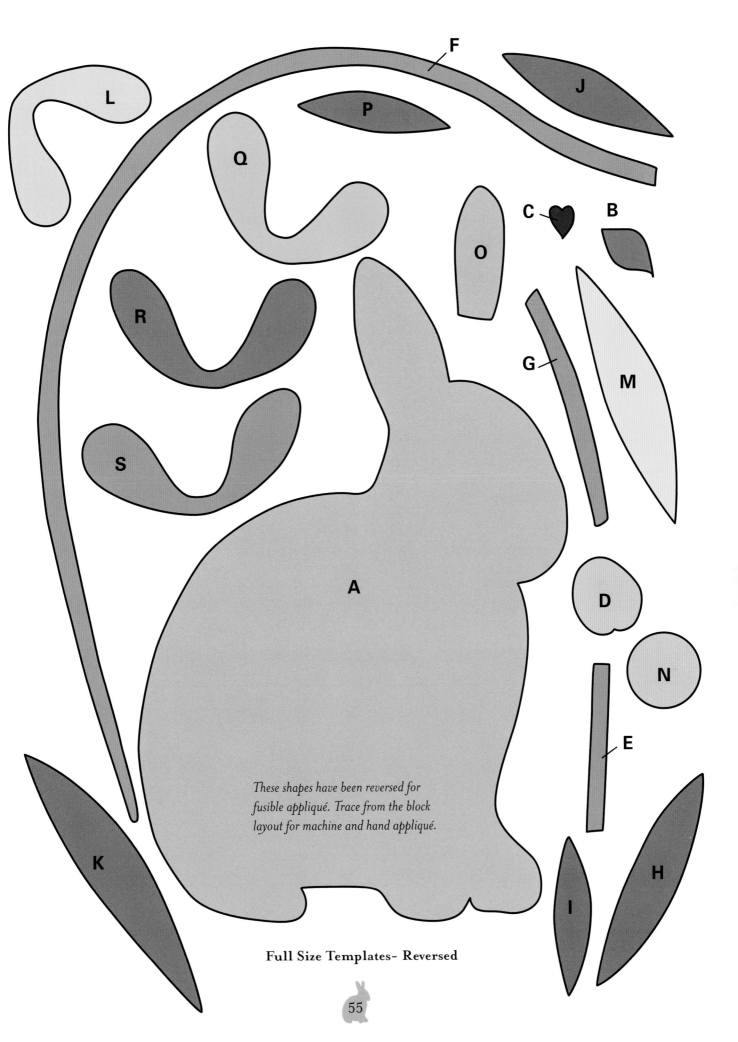

These shapes have been reversed for fusible appliqué. Trace from the block layout for machine and hand appliqué.

Full Size Templates- Reversed

Block 6 - Buds in Bloom

EACH OF THE FOUR STEMS SHOWCASES TWO ELEGANT FLOWERS
THAT ARE FUSSY-CUT INSIDE A YET-TO-BLOOM BUD IN AN
ARTFULLY ARRANGED BOUQUET.

Note: Diagram not to scale; for color placement only.

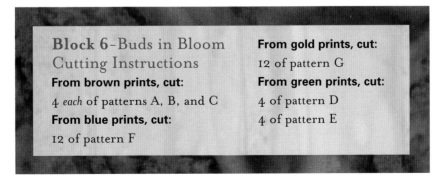

Block 6-Buds in Bloom
Cutting Instructions

From brown prints, cut:
4 *each* of patterns A, B, and C

From blue prints, cut:
12 of pattern F

From gold prints, cut:
12 of pattern G

From green prints, cut:
4 of pattern D
4 of pattern E

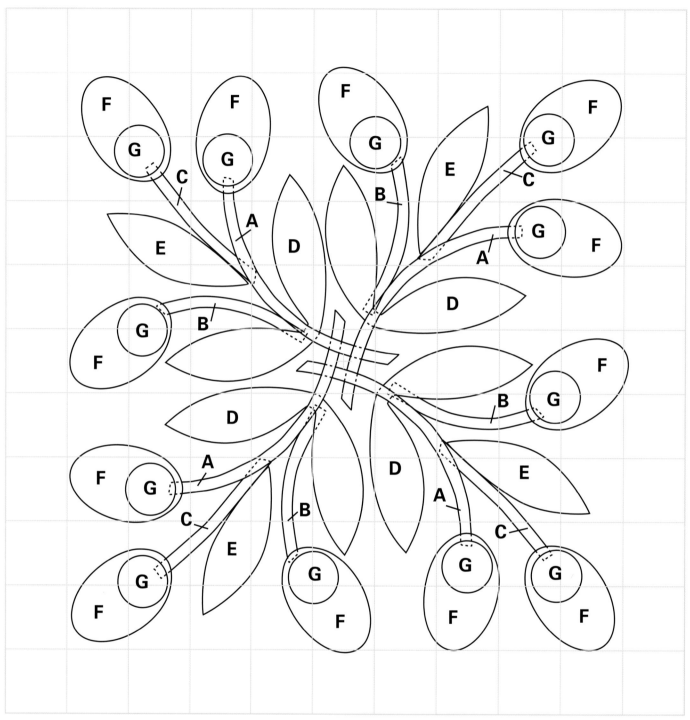

I square equals I inch

For machine and hand appliqué enlarge the block layout and trace shapes exactly. Do not reverse.

Enlarge 150%

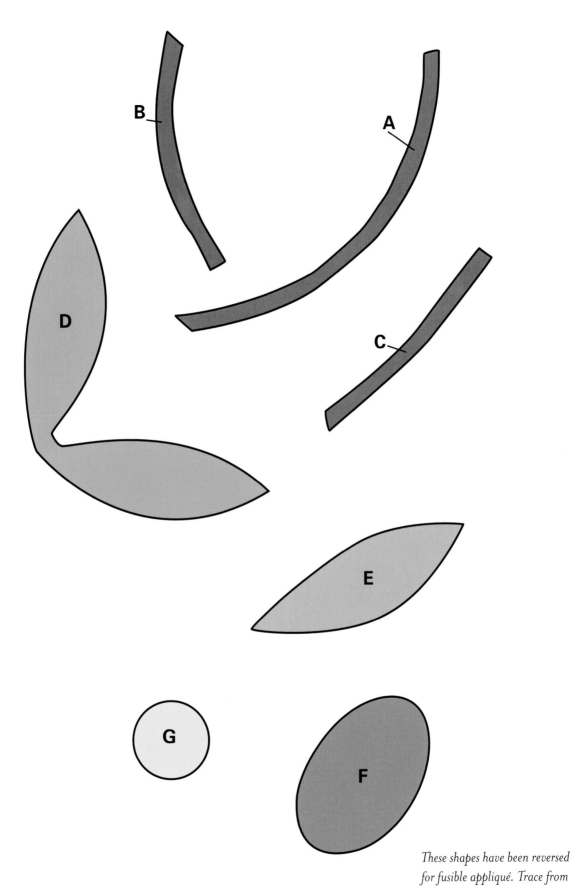

Full Size Templates- Reversed

These shapes have been reversed for fusible appliqué. Trace from the block layout for machine and hand appliqué.

Block 7 - Batik Beauty

ATTENTION CENTERS ON THE BATIK FLORAL SHAPE RHYTHMICALLY PLACED BETWEEN BUDS THAT ARE MIRROR-IMAGED ON EITHER SIDE OF A GRACEFUL CENTER.

Note: Diagram not to scale; for color placement only.

Block 7–Batik Beauty
Cutting Instructions

From brown prints, cut:
1 *each* of patterns H, Hr, I, Ir, J, and Jr

From red prints, cut:
1 of pattern B
2 of pattern D

From blue prints, cut:
1 of pattern A
2 *each* of patterns D and G

From green prints, cut:
4 *each* of pattern C
1 *each* of patterns E, Er, F, Fr, K, and Kr

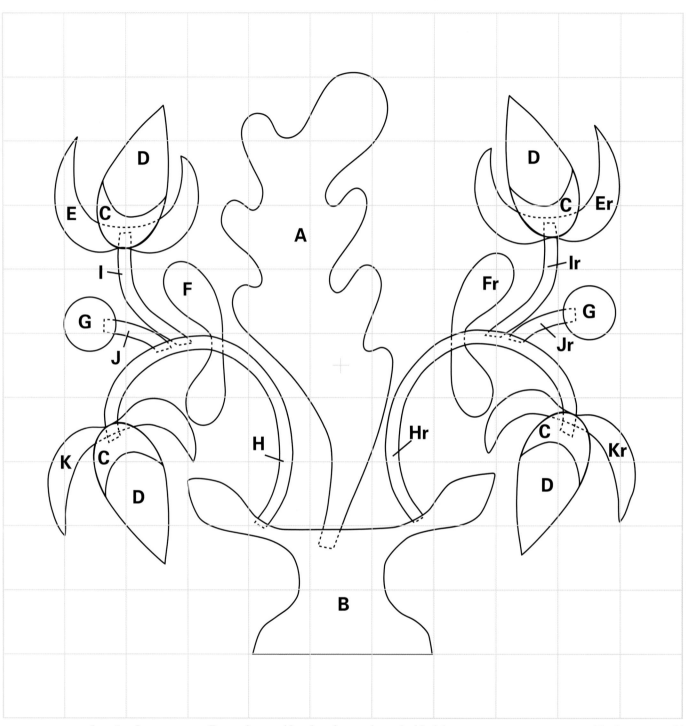

1 square equals 1 inch

For machine and hand appliqué enlarge the block layout and trace shapes exactly. Do not reverse.

Enlarge 150%

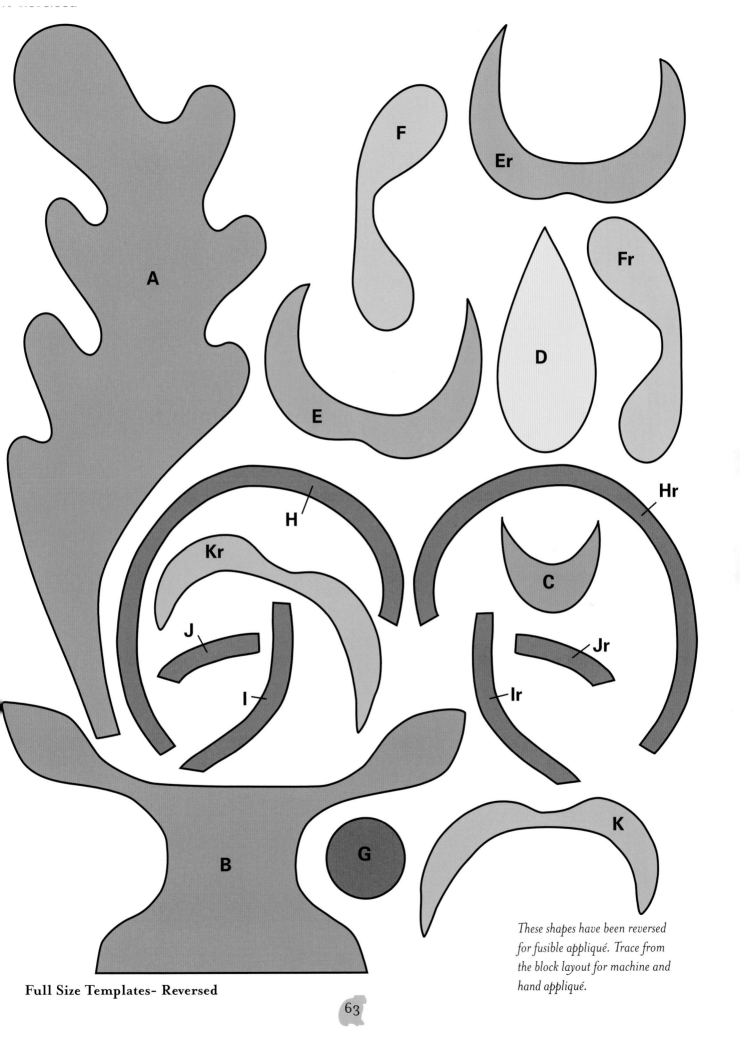

Full Size Templates- Reversed

These shapes have been reversed for fusible appliqué. Trace from the block layout for machine and hand appliqué.

Block 8 - Lily Dreams

LET YOUR IMAGINATION PLAY IN A FIELD WHERE PURPLE-HUED
LILY PETALS ENTWINE BRANCHING LEAVES AND ORANGE BUDS.

Note: Diagram not to scale; for color placement only.

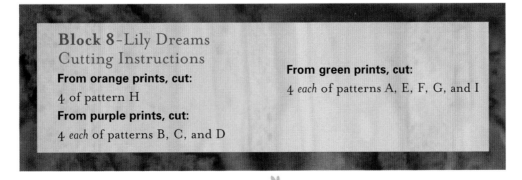

Block 8-Lily Dreams
Cutting Instructions

From orange prints, cut:
4 of pattern H

From purple prints, cut:
4 *each* of patterns B, C, and D

From green prints, cut:
4 *each* of patterns A, E, F, G, and I

I square equals I inch

For machine and hand appliqué enlarge the block layout
and trace shapes exactly. Do not reverse.

Enlarge 150%

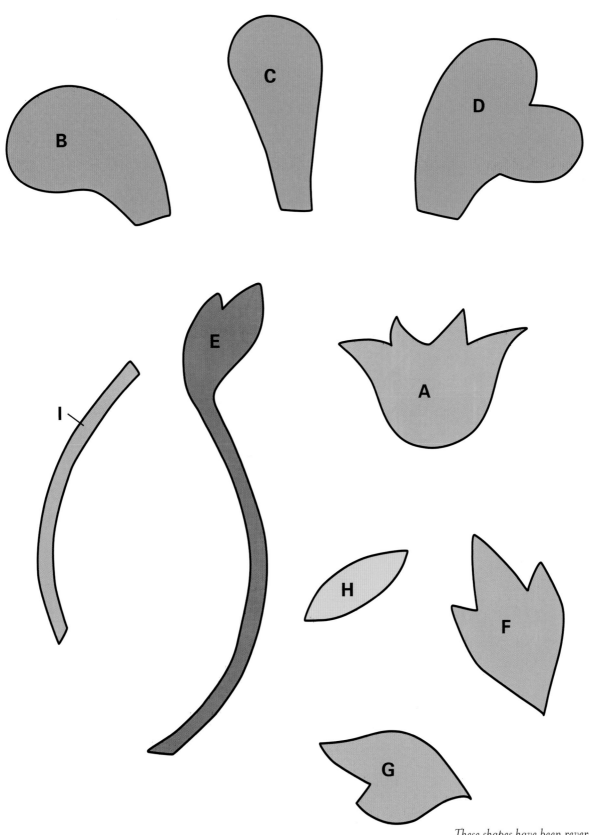

These shapes have been reversed for fusible appliqué. Trace from the block layout for machine and hand appliqué.

Full Size Templates- Reversed

Block 9 - Garden Grace

THE USE OF COLOR SHADING AND THE RULE OF FIVE FABRIC
PATTERNS ARE DISPLAYED IN THIS SIMPLE AND EFFECTIVE FLORAL
VASE ARRANGEMENT.

Note: Diagram not to scale; for color placement only.

Block 9–Garden Grace
Cutting Instructions

From brown prints, cut:

1 *each* of patterns B, Br, and C

From red prints, cut:

1 of pattern F

From blue prints, cut:

2 of pattern I

2 of pattern J

2 of pattern G

From gold prints, cut:

11 of pattern H

From green prints, cut:

1 of pattern A

2 *each* of patterns D, E, L, and M

1 of pattern K

I square equals I inch

For machine and hand appliqué enlarge the block layout and trace shapes exactly. Do not reverse.

Enlarge 150%

J

G

E

I

C

L

Br

B

M

H

K

F

A

D

Full Size Templates- Reversed

These shapes have been reversed for fusible appliqué. Trace from the block layout for machine and hand appliqué.

Block 10 – Enchanted Garden

INTRODUCING DISTINCTIVE BLACK FABRIC WITH PATTERNS PICKS UP THE COLOR PALETTE OF THE QUILT AND ADDS A FRESH NOTE OF INTEREST. THE HUES OF THE BATIK FLOWERS REFLECT THE COLORS OF THE FUSSY-CUT DESIGNS WITHIN THE BLACK PETALS.

Note: Diagram not to scale; for color placement only.

Block 10-Enchanted Garden
Cutting Instructions

From brown prints, cut:

4 of pattern I

4 of pattern J

4 of pattern K

From red prints, cut:

4 *each* of patterns C, D, E, F, and G

From gold prints, cut:

4 of pattern B

From green prints, cut:

4 of pattern A

8 of pattern H

1 square equals 1 inch

For machine and hand appliqué enlarge the block layout and trace shapes exactly. Do not reverse.

Enlarge 150%

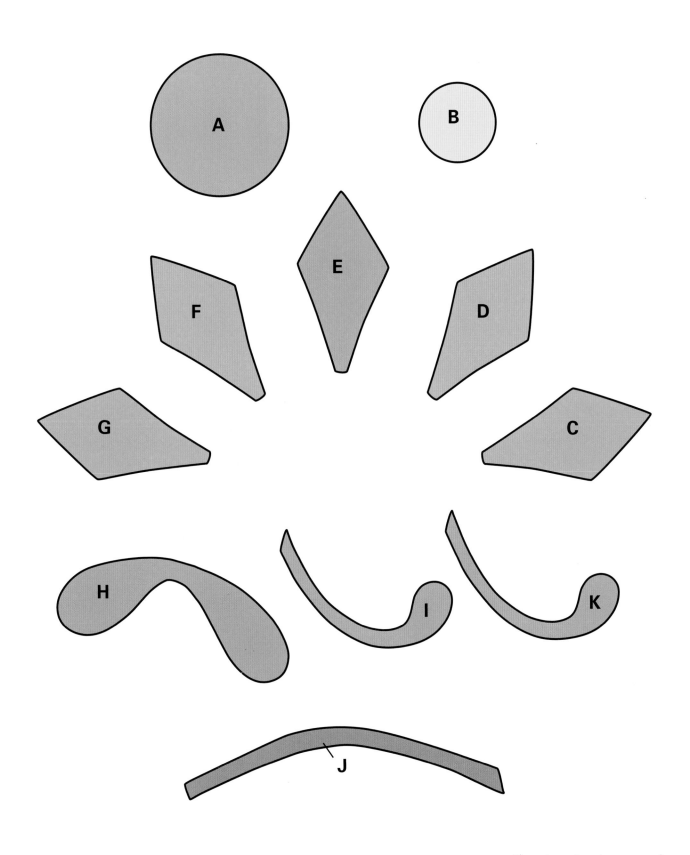

Full Size Templates- Reversed

These shapes have been reversed for fusible appliqué. Trace from the block layout for machine and hand appliqué.

From My Garden Album Quilt

Block II - Spring Breezes

MOTION IS EVERYWHERE—FROM THE ARCHED STEMS TO THE SUGGESTION OF LEAVES IN THE BREEZE AGAINST A BACKGROUND OF SOFT UNDULATING STRIPES.

Note: Diagram not to scale; for color placement only.

Block 11-Spring Breezes
Cutting Instructions

From brown prints, cut:
4 of pattern F

From orange prints, cut:
4 of pattern A

From blue prints, cut:
4 *each* of patterns D and Dr

From gold prints, cut:
8 of pattern E

From green prints, cut:
4 *each* of patterns B and C

I square equals I inch

For machine and hand appliqué enlarge the block layout and trace shapes exactly. Do not reverse.

Enlarge 150%

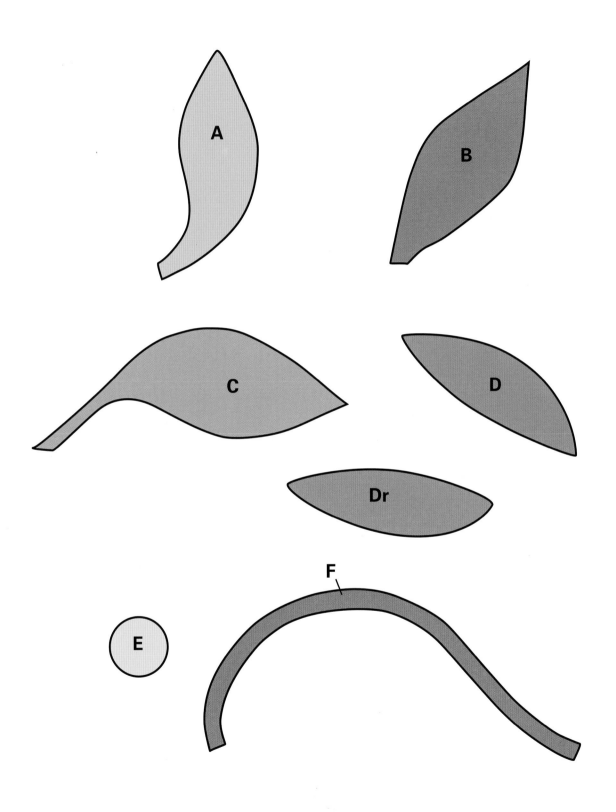

Full Size Templates- Reversed

These shapes have been reversed for fusible appliqué. Trace from the block layout for machine and hand appliqué.

Block 12 - Rose Hip Wreath

PERHAPS THE MOST TRADITIONAL OF THE BLOCKS, THE ROSE HIP WREATH BLOCK REPEATS FOUR DESIGN ELEMENTS, EACH BALANCED WITH FUSSY-CUT PINK BUDS AND SHADES OF GREEN LEAVES ON A CONNECTING VINE.

Note: Diagram not to scale; for color placement only.

Block 12-Rose Hip Wreath
Cutting Instructions

From brown prints, cut:

4 of pattern G

8 of pattern H

From red prints, cut:

8 *each* of patterns C and D

4 of pattern E

From gold prints, cut:

4 of pattern F

From green prints, cut:

8 of pattern B

4 *each* of patterns A and I

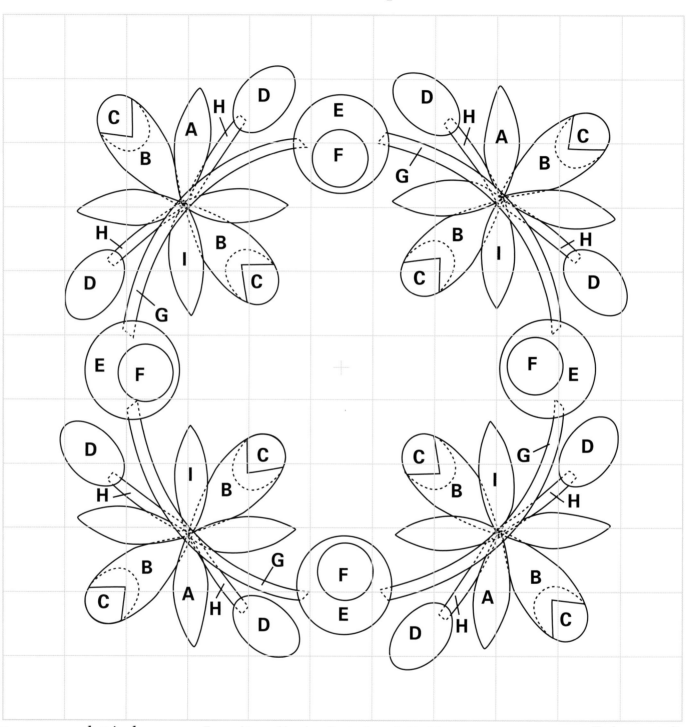

1 square equals 1 inch

For machine and hand appliqué enlarge the block layout and trace shapes exactly. Do not reverse.

Enlarge 150%

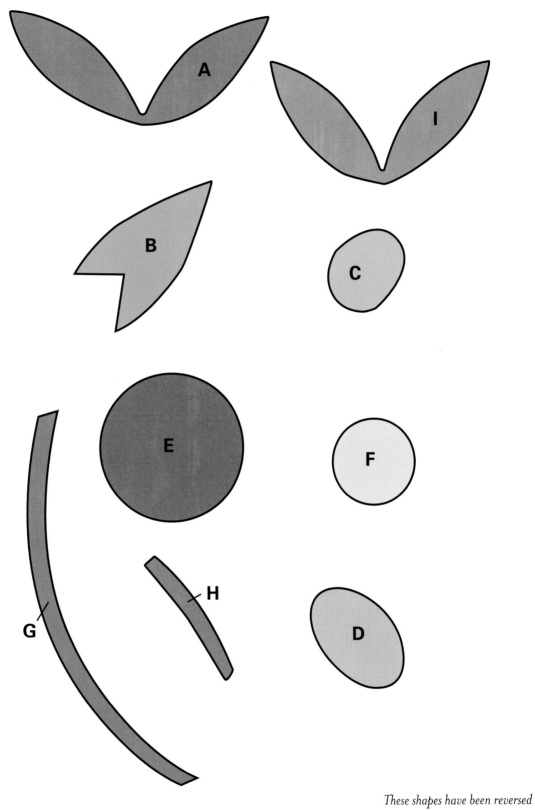

Letter labels on the templates: A, I, B, C, E, F, G, H, D

These shapes have been reversed for fusible appliqué. Trace from the block layout for machine and hand appliqué.

Full Size Templates- Reversed

Assemble the Sashing

1. Referring to the diagram, lay out two off-white and two assorted warm color (yellow, orange, red, rust, purple) sashing triangles. Sew the triangles together in pairs. Press the seams toward the warm color triangles. Join the pairs together to make one hourglass unit. Press the seams in one direction. Each pieced hourglass unit should measure $3^{3}/_{8}$" square. Repeat to make a total of 124 hourglass units.

Make 124

2. Sew four hourglass units together in a row to make a sashing unit. Press the seam allowances open. The pieced sashing unit should measure $3^{3}/_{8}$" x 12". Repeat to make a total of 31 sashing units.

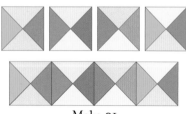

Make 31

3. Sew together one off-white corner sashing triangle and one warm color (yellow, orange, red, rust, purple) corner sashing triangle to make a corner sashing unit. Press the seam allowance toward the orange triangle. The pieced corner sashing unit should measure $3^{3}/_{8}$" square. Repeat to make a total of four corner sashing units.

Make 4

Assemble the Quilt Center

1. Referring to the Quilt Center Assembly Diagram lay out the 12 appliquéd blocks, sashing units, corner sashing units, and batik sashing squares in nine horizontal rows.

2. Sew the pieces together in each row. Press the seam allowances toward the sashing units.

3. Join the rows to make the quilt center. The pieced quilt center should measure $46^{1}/_{2}$" x $60^{7}/_{8}$".

Add the Borders

1. Piece the multi-color batik $3^{3}/_{8}$" x 44" strips to make the following:
   2—$3^{3}/_{8}$" x 55" for top and bottom
   2—$3^{3}/_{8}$" x 69" for sides

2. Center and add the inner border strips to the quilt center mitering the corners. The quilt center should now measure $52^{1}/_{4}$" x $66^{5}/_{8}$".

3. Piece the dark green batik $6^{3}/_{8}$" x 44" strips to make the following:
   2—$6^{3}/_{8}$" x $66^{5}/_{8}$" strips for sides
   2—$6^{3}/_{8}$" x 64" strips for top and bottom

4. Add the side outer border strips to the quilt top. Press the seams toward the outer border. Add the top and bottom outer border strips to the quilt top. Press the seams toward the outer border.

Complete the Quilt

1. Layer the quilt top.

2. Quilt as desired.

3. Bind the quilt with the light green batik strips.

Quilt Center Assembly Diagram

The Projects

Individual blocks in the
From My Garden Album Quilt
inspire beautiful quilt
projects. Be creative and
substitute your favorite
block for even more variety.

Materials

- 13" x 14" rectangle light beige-grey batik for appliqué foundation
- ⅜ yard blue-and-brown print for inner border
- ¼ yard brown tone-on-tone for middle border
- ½ yard dark green batik for outer border
- ¼ yard multi-color batik for binding
- 6" x 8" rectangle blue-grey print for body, ear and mouth appliqués
- 8" x 9" rectangle brown print for stem appliqués
- 5" square red print for leaf appliqués
- 5 assorted green print and batik scraps for leaf appliqués
- 2 assorted gold batik scraps for leaf appliqués
- Pink print scrap for flower appliqués
- Solid black scrap for eye and nose appliqués
- 28" x 29" backing fabric
- 28" x 29" batting

Finished appliqué block: 10½" x 11½"
Finished wallhanging: 21½" x 23"

Quantities are for 44/45"-wide, 100% cotton fabrics. Measurements include ¼" seam allowances. Sew with right sides together unless otherwise stated.

Cut the Fabrics

From blue-and-brown print, cut:
4–2¼" x 42" inner border strips
From brown tone-on-tone, cut:
4–1¼" x 42" middle border strips
From dark green batik, cut:
4–3¼" x 42" outer border strips
From multi-color batik, cut:
3–2½" x 42" binding strips

Cut and Assemble the Appliqué Block

1. Use the appliqué method of your choice on pages 18–31 and the patterns on pages 54–55 to prepare the appliqué pieces.

From blue-grey print, cut:
1 each of patterns A, D, and O
From brown print, cut:
1 each of patterns E, F, and G
From red print, cut:
1 each of patterns H, I, J, K, and P

From green prints and batik scraps, cut:
2 of pattern Q
1 each of patterns L, R, and S
From gold batik scraps, cut:
1 of pattern L
1 of pattern M
From pink print scrap, cut:
3 of pattern N
From solid black scrap, cut:
1 each of patterns B and C

2. Position the appliqué pieces on the 13" x 14" light beige-grey batik foundation rectangle. Appliqué the shapes in place using your favorite method. Press the appliquéd block from the back. Center and trim it to 11" x 12".

Garden Guest Wallhanging

Assemble the Wallhanging Top

1. Sew together a blue-and-brown print inner border strip, a brown tone-on-tone middle border strip, and a dark green batik outer border strip to make a border unit. Press seams toward the outer border. Repeat to make a second border unit.

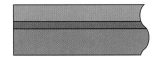

Make 2

2. Cut two 25" lengths from the border units. With right sides together sew the units to the top and bottom edges of the block, beginning and ending seams $\frac{1}{4}$" from the block corners.

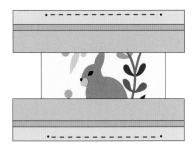

3. Repeat Step 1, pressing seams toward the inner border. Cut two 26" lengths from the border units. With right sides together, sew the units to the remaining edges of the block, beginning and ending seams $\frac{1}{4}$" from the block corners.

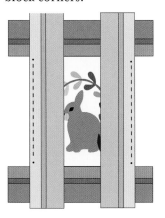

4. Refer to mitering corners to complete the wallhanging top.

Mitering Corners

1. Working on a flat surface, lay out the wallhanging with one border laying vertically.

2. Bring the adjoining border up and fold at a 45-degree angle. It should lay on top of the border in Step 1. Press.

3. Fold the wallhanging center on the diagonal, right sides together.

4. The pressed border should now be laying flat on top of the other border strip. Pin along creased line.

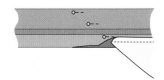

5. Stitch on the creased line, backstitching $\frac{1}{4}$" from the edges. Trim seam to $\frac{1}{4}$". Press.

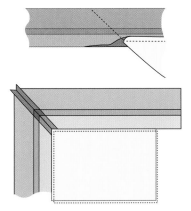

6. Repeat for remaining corners.

Complete the Wallhanging

1. Layer wallhanging top, batting, and backing.

2. Quilt as desired. The Garden Guest wallhanging was stitched in-the-ditch of every border seam, then $\frac{1}{4}$" inside the first stitching on the block and middle border. To add dimension to the appliquéd block, it was machine-stitched around all the appliqués and echo-quilted $\frac{1}{4}$" beyond the shapes. The inner border has a stippling stitch and a leaf pattern was added over the outer border.

3. Bind with multi-color batik binding strips.

Garden Guest Wallhanging

Designed and pieced by Edyta Sitar; machine quilted by Julie Lillo

Garden Table Runner

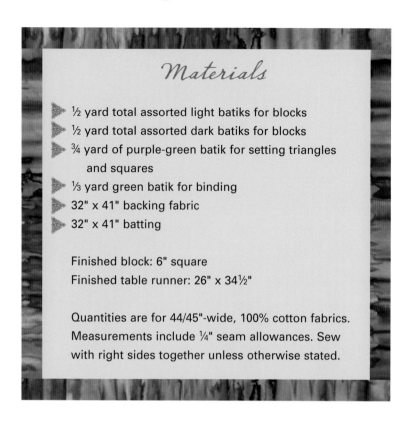

Materials

➤ ½ yard total assorted light batiks for blocks

➤ ½ yard total assorted dark batiks for blocks

➤ ¾ yard of purple-green batik for setting triangles and squares

➤ ⅓ yard green batik for binding

➤ 32" x 41" backing fabric

➤ 32" x 41" batting

Finished block: 6" square
Finished table runner: 26" x 34½"

Quantities are for 44/45"-wide, 100% cotton fabrics. Measurements include ¼" seam allowances. Sew with right sides together unless otherwise stated.

Cut the Fabrics

Cut pieces in the following order.

From assorted light batiks, cut:
33–1½" x 12" strips
From assorted dark batiks, cut:
33–1½" x 12" strips
From purple-green batik, cut:
7–9¾" squares, cutting each diagonally in an X for a total of 28 setting triangles
2–6½" squares
From green batik, cut:
4–2½" x 42" binding strips

Assemble the Blocks

1. Aligning long edges, sew together three light batik strips and three dark batik strips to make a strip set as shown. Press seams toward the dark strips. Repeat to make a total of 11 strip sets. Cut six 1½"-wide segments from each strip set for a total of 66 segments.

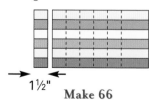

← 1½" →
Make 66

2. Randomly sew together six segments, alternating the direction of the segments to achieve a checkerboard pattern with the light and dark batiks.

Press seams in one direction. The block should be 6½" square. Repeat to make 11 blocks.

Make 11

Assemble the Rows

1. Sew purple-green batik setting triangles to opposite edges of each block to make a Block-Triangle unit as shown. Press seams toward the setting triangles. Repeat to make 11 Block-Triangle units.

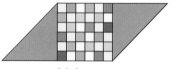

Make 11

2. Carefully matching seams, sew together four Block-Triangle units in a row. Press seams in one direction. Add a purple-green batik setting triangle to each end to make Row A. Press seams toward the setting triangles. Repeat to make a second Row A.

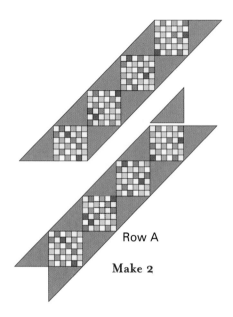

Row A

Make 2

3. Sew a setting triangle to each 6½" purple-green batik square to make a Square-Triangle unit. Press seams toward setting triangles.

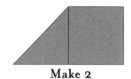

Make 2

4. Join the three remaining Block-Triangle units in a row, carefully matching seams. Press seams in one direction. Add a Square-Triangle unit to each end to make Row B. Press seams toward the Square-Triangle units.

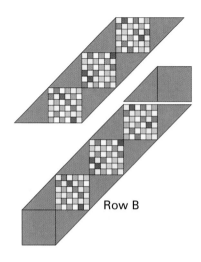

Row B

5. Referring to Table Runner Assembly Diagram, lay out alternating A and B rows. Join rows to complete runner top. Press seams in one direction.

Note: Trim the table runner top after it has been quilted to prevent distortion.

Complete the Table Runner

1. Layer table runner top, batting, and backing.

2. Quilt as desired. The table runner is stitched with an orange-peel-style design in each block. The purple-green vertical rows were outlined, stitching ¼" inside the seam lines, and the rows are filled with stippling.

3. Trim the table runner ¼" beyond points of blocks in A rows.

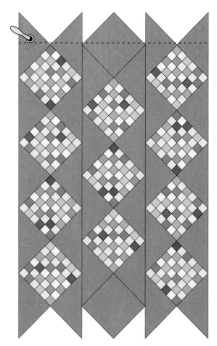

Table Runner Assembly Diagram

4. Bind with green batik binding strips.

Garden Table Runner

Designed and pieced by Edyta Sitar; machine quilted by Julie Lillo

Spring Reel Table Topper

Materials

- 9–12" squares of assorted light prints for appliqué foundations
- ¾ yard light multi-color batik for border
- ½ yard dark multi-color batik for binding
- 9–8" squares of assorted red, orange, brown or multi-color prints and batiks for spoke appliqués
- 9–6" squares of assorted blue prints and batiks for petal appliqués
- 5–6" x 8" rectangles of assorted green prints and batiks for leaf appliqués
- 7–8" squares of assorted gold prints and batiks for petal and spoke center appliqués
- 2⅝ yards backing fabric
- 47" square batting

Finished appliqué block: 9½" square
Finished table topper: 41" square

Quantities are for 44/45"-wide, 100% cotton fabrics. Measurements include ¼" seam allowances. Sew with right sides together unless otherwise stated.

Cut the Fabrics

From light multi-color batik, cut:
2–6½" x 29" border strips
2–6½" x 41" border strips
From dark multi-color batik, cut:
5–2½" x 42" binding strips
From backing, cut:
2–24" x 47" rectangles

Cut and Assemble the Appliqué Blocks

1. Trace the appliqué patterns from pages 100-101. Use the appliqué method of your choice on pages 18-31 to prepare appliqué pieces.

From red, orange, brown or multi-color prints and batiks, cut:
9 of pattern A
From blue prints and batiks, cut:
36 *each* of patterns E and F
From green prints and batiks, cut:
32 of pattern C
From gold prints and batiks, cut:
9 of pattern B
4 of pattern C
36 of pattern D

2. Position one set of appliqué pieces on each 12" assorted light print foundation square. Appliqué the shapes in place using your favorite method. Press appliquéd blocks from the back. Center and trim each to a 10" square.

Note: The fabrics in the Spring Reel table topper vary from block to block, sometimes using all the same fabric on one block for a leaf or petal shape and sometimes using up to four different fabrics for the same shape.

Spring Reel Table Topper

Assemble the Table Topper

1. Lay out nine blocks in three rows, referring to the Table Topper Center Assembly Diagram.

2. Sew the blocks in each row together. Press seams in one direction, alternating each row's direction.

3. Join rows to make the table topper center. Press seams in one direction. The topper center should be 29" square.

4. Referring to the Table Topper Assembly Diagram, sew $6\frac{1}{2}$" x 29" border strips to opposite edges of the topper center. Press seams toward the border. Add $6\frac{1}{2}$" x 4" border strips to remaining edges. Press seams toward the border.

Complete the Table Topper

1. Sew together the 24" x 47" backing rectangles along one long edge, using a $\frac{1}{2}$" seam allowance. Press the seam allowance open.

2. Layer top, batting, and pieced backing.

3. Quilt as desired. The table topper was stitched closely around the appliqué shapes and then echo-quilted approximately $\frac{1}{4}$" outside the first stitching. A feathered vine was added in the border that overlaps the blocks. An all-over pebble design was used to fill in the background of the blocks and border.

4. Bind with dark multi-color batik binding strips.

Table Topper Center Assembly Diagram

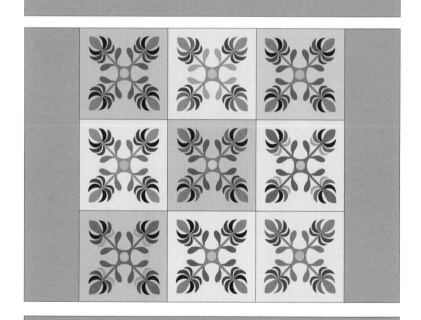

Table Topper Assembly Diagram

98

Spring Reel Table Topper

Designed and pieced by Edyta Sitar; machine quilted by Julie Lillo

Spring Reel Table Topper

Full Size Block Layout

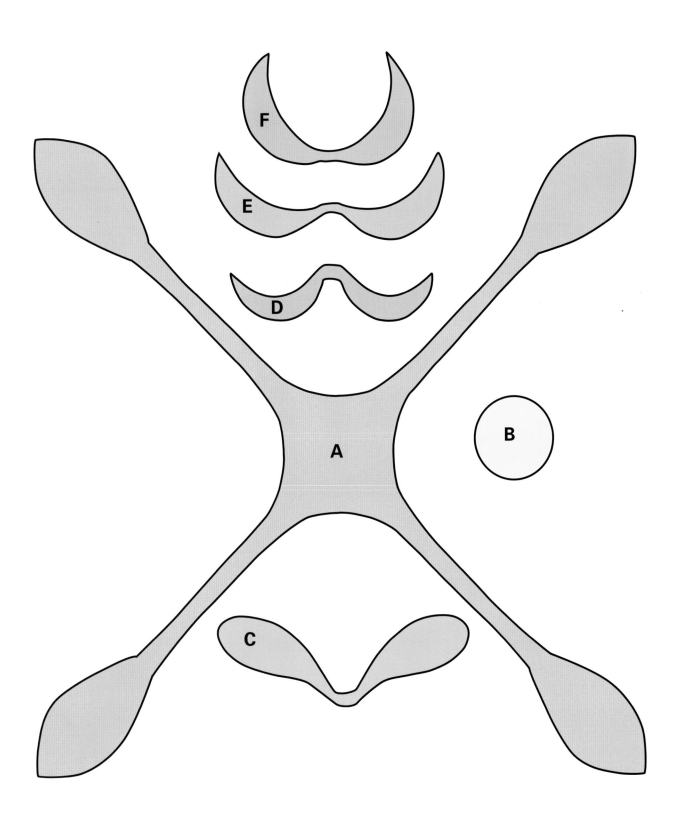

F

E

D

A

B

C

These shapes have been reversed for fusible appliqué.
Trace from the block layout for machine and hand appliqué

Full Size Templates

Batik Beauty Pillow

Materials

- 14½" x 14" rectangle cream-and-beige batik for appliqué foundation
- ⅝ yard multi-color pattern batik for outer border and back
- ⅛ yard or fat-eighth gold batik for inner border
- 4" x 8" rectangle blue batik for plume appliqué
- 4" x 6" rectangle brown-and-red print for urn appliqué
- 8" square brown print for stem appliqués
- 4 assorted green print and batik scraps for leaf and flower base appliqués
- 2 assorted blue print and batik scraps for flower appliqués
- Peach batik scrap for flower appliqués
- 42" x 22" backing fabric
- 42" x 22" batting
- Pillow form

Finished appliqué block: 12" x 11½"
Finished pillow cover: 16" x 15"

Quantities are for 44/45" wide, 100% cotton fabrics. Measurements include ¼" seam allowances. Sew with right sides together unless otherwise stated.

Cut the Fabric

From multi-color pattern batik, cut:
2—12½" x 15½" outer border/back rectangles
2—2¼" x 12½" outer border strips
2—2½" x 15½" binding strips

From gold batik, cut:
2—1½" x 12" inner border strips
2—1½" x 12½" inner border strips

Cut and Assemble the Appliqué Block

1. Use the appliqué method of your choice on pages 18-31 and the patterns on pages 62-63 to prepare the appliqué pieces.

From blue batik, cut:
1 of pattern A
From brown-and-red print, cut:
1 of pattern B

From brown print, cut:
1 *each* of patterns H, Hr, I, Ir, J, and Jr
From assorted green prints and batik scraps, cut:
4 of pattern C
1 *each* of patterns E, Er, F, Fr, K, and Kr
From blue prints and batik scraps, cut:
2 *each* of patterns D and G
From peach batik scrap, cut:
2 of pattern D

2. Position the appliqué pieces on the 14½" x 14" cream-and-beige batik foundation rectangle and appliqué the shapes in place using your favorite method. Press appliquéd block from the back. Center and trim to 12½" x 12".

Batik Beauty Pillow

Assemble the Pillow Cover

1. With wrong sides together, fold each gold batik inner border strip in half lengthwise to measure $3/4$"-wide; press.

2. Position the 12" inner border strips on the front of the appliqué block, aligning the raw edges of the strips with the side edges of the block. Baste in place. Repeat with the $12^1/2$" inner border strips along the top and bottom edges of the block.

3. Referring to the diagram, sew the multi-color batik $2^1/4$" x $12^1/2$" outer border strips to the top and bottom edges of the block. Press seams toward outer border.

4. Sew the multi-color $12^1/2$" x $15^1/2$" outer border/back rectangles to the side edges of the block. Press seams toward the outer border/back.

Complete the Pillow Cover

1. Layer pillow cover top, batting, and backing.

2. Quilt as desired. The pillow cover was stitched in-the-ditch of the block. To add dimension, it was stitched closely around the appliqué shapes and echo-quilted $1/4$" and $1/2$" outside the first stitching. A 1" grid was added over the border and back pieces. The background of the block has an all-over pebble design.

3. Bind the remaining $15^1/2$" edges of the border/back rectangles with the multi-color batik $2^1/2$" x $15^1/2$" binding strips.

4. Trim the batting and backing even with the top and bottom edges of the pillow cover.

5. With right sides together, fold the quilted rectangle to overlap the bound edges about 4" at the center back, creating a $2^1/4$"-wide border on the front; pin. Sew together along the top and bottom edges to make the cover. Trim corners, turn right side out, and press. Insert the pillow form.

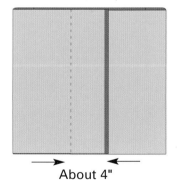

About 4"

Batik Beauty Pillow

Designed and pieced by Edyta Sitar; machine quilted by Julie Lillo

Fleur Delight Throw

Cut the Fabrics

Cut pieces in the following order.

From turquoise batik, cut:
4–10" squares
16–5¼" squares

From assorted gold, pink, and purple batiks, cut:
4–10" squares from each of five batiks for a total of 20 squares
2–10" squares from each of two remaining batiks for a total of 4 squares

From green batik, cut:
16–5¼" squares

From brown batik, cut:
12–5¼" squares

From blue batik, cut:
4–5¼" squares

From brown-blue batik, cut:
4–15" squares, cutting each diagonally in an X for a total of 16 setting triangles
2–8" squares, cutting each in half diagonally for a total of 4 corner triangles

From multi-color batik, cut:
7–2½" x 42" binding strips

From backing fabric, cut:
2–37" x 73" rectangles

Cut and Assemble the Appliqué Block

1. Use the appliqué method of your choice on pages 18-31 and the patterns on page 42-43 to prepare appliqué pieces.

From brown prints and batiks, cut:
1 *each* of patterns A, B, and C
3 of pattern E

From green prints and batik scraps, cut:
1 *each* of patterns D, F, G, and M
3 of pattern I
2 *each* of patterns J and L

From blue print scraps, cut:
3 of pattern H

From pink print scrap, cut:
3 of pattern K

2. Position the appliqué pieces on the 12" light print foundation square, adjusting the placement as needed to keep the pieces within a 9½" square area at the center of the square. Appliqué the shapes in place using your favorite method. Press appliquéd block from the back. Center and trim to 10" square.

Fleur Delight Throw

Assemble the Throw Top

1. Lay out four $5\frac{1}{4}$" squares as shown. Refer to the photograph for color placement ideas.

Note: A brown batik square was used in each block. The other fabrics vary from block to block, sometimes using two green or two turquoise in a block.

2. Sew the squares together in pairs. Press seams in opposite directions. Join pairs to make a four-patch block measuring 10" square. Press seams in one direction. Repeat to make 12 four-patch blocks.

Make 12

3. Referring to Throw Assembly Diagram, lay out appliqué block, 28–10" squares, 12 four-patch blocks, and 16 brown-blue batik setting triangles in diagonal rows.

4. Sew together pieces in each row. Press seams in one direction, alternating the direction with each row.

5. Join rows; press seams in one direction. Add brown-blue batik corner triangles to complete the quilt top. Press seams toward corner triangles.

Complete the Throw

1. Sew together the 37" x 73" backing rectangles along one long edge, using a $\frac{1}{2}$" seam allowance. Press the seam allowance open.

2. Layer throw top, batting, and pieced backing.

3. Quilt as desired. The throw is stitched in-the-ditch of the appliqué block and then closely around each shape and $\frac{1}{4}$" beyond the shapes. A swirl pattern was stitched over the remainder of the throw top.

4. Bind with multi-color batik binding strips.

Throw Assembly Diagram

Fleur Delight Throw

Designed and pieced by Edyta Sitar; machine quilted by Julie Lillo

Starscape Quilt

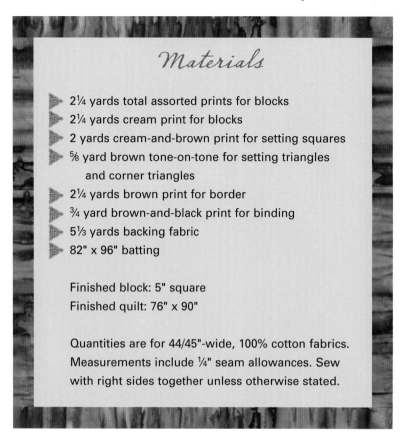

Materials

- 2¼ yards total assorted prints for blocks
- 2¼ yards cream print for blocks
- 2 yards cream-and-brown print for setting squares
- ⅝ yard brown tone-on-tone for setting triangles and corner triangles
- 2¼ yards brown print for border
- ¾ yard brown-and-black print for binding
- 5⅓ yards backing fabric
- 82" x 96" batting

Finished block: 5" square
Finished quilt: 76" x 90"

Quantities are for 44/45"-wide, 100% cotton fabrics. Measurements include ¼" seam allowances. Sew with right sides together unless otherwise stated.

Cut the Fabrics

Cut pieces in the following order. Border strips are exact length needed. You may want to make them longer to allow for variations in piecing.

From assorted prints, cut:

50—1½" x 42" strips; cut each strip into sixteen 1½" diamonds for a total of 800 diamonds (see Cutting Diamonds).

From cream print, cut:

396—2⅛" squares

99—3½" squares, cutting each diagonally in an X for a total of 396 small triangles

From cream-and-brown print, cut:

80—5½" setting squares

From brown tone-on-tone, cut:

9—8¼" squares, cutting each diagonally in an X for a total of 36 setting triangles

2—4½" squares, cutting each in half diagonally for a total of 4 corner triangles

From brown print, cut:

2—6½" x 78" border strips

2—6½" x 76" border strips

From brown-and-black print, cut:

9—2½" x 42" binding strips

From backing fabric, cut:

2—42" x 96" rectangles

Cutting Diamonds

Trim end of 1½"-wide strip at a 45-degree angle. Place the 1½" line of ruler along the angled edge of the strip. Cut along edge of ruler to make one diamond. Continue in this manner to cut 16 diamonds from each strip (4 sets of 4).

Marking Diamonds

For ease in piecing the Eight-Pointed Star blocks, you may find it helpful to mark the diamonds, squares, and triangles. Use a ruler and pencil to lightly draw a line or dot to indicate the starting and stopping points for the ¼" set-in seams.

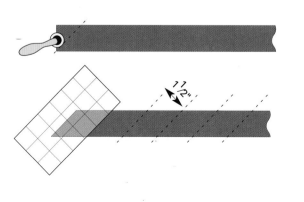

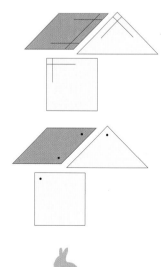

Starscape Quilt

Assemble the Blocks

1. For one Eight-Pointed Star block you will need four matching diamonds from one print, four matching diamonds from a second print, four cream print $2^{1}/8$" squares, and four cream print small triangles.

2. Sew together a diamond from each print to make a diamond pair, taking care not to sew into the $^{1}/4$" seam allowance. Backstitch to secure seam ends. Press seam toward darker diamond.

3. Pin a cream print small triangle to one diamond in the diamond pair; the triangle will extend slightly beyond the outer points of the diamond. Sew from the inner corner to the outside edge, backstitching at the inner corner to secure. Pin the adjacent diamond in the pair to the triangle. Sew from inner corner to outside edge to make a star point unit. Press seams toward the diamonds.

4. Repeat Steps 2 and 3 to make a total of four matching star point units.

5. Join two star point units, making sure you don't sew into the $^{1}/4$" seam allowance. Sew a cream print $2^{1}/8$" square into the corner between the star point units to make a star half; square will extend slightly beyond outer edges of star half. Press seams toward diamonds. Repeat to make a second star half.

6. Sew together two star halves without sewing into the $^{1}/4$" seam allowance. Sew cream print $2^{1}/8$" squares into remaining corners to make an Eight-Pointed Star block. Press seams toward the diamonds. Trim block to $5^{1}/2$" square.

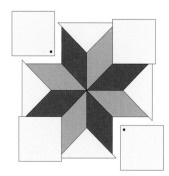

7. Repeat Steps 1-6 to make a total of 99 Eight-Pointed Star blocks. You will use 198 sets of 4 matching diamonds (792 diamonds total) to make the 99 blocks. There will be 8 unused diamonds.

Assemble the Quilt Center

1. Referring to Quilt Center Assembly Diagram, lay out Eight-Pointed Star blocks, cream-and-brown print setting squares, and brown tone-on-tone setting triangles in diagonal rows.

2. Sew together pieces in each row. Press seams toward setting pieces.

3. Join rows. Press seams in one direction. Add brown tone-on-tone corner triangles to complete the quilt center. Press seams toward the corner triangles. The quilt center should measure approximately 64" x 78".

Add the Border

1. Referring to Quilt Top Assembly Diagram, sew $6^{1}/2$" x 78" border strips to long edges of the quilt center. Press seams toward border.

2. Add $6^{1}/2$" x 76" border strips to remaining edges. Press seams toward border.

Complete the Quilt

1. Sew together the 42" x 96" backing rectangles along one long edge, using a $\frac{1}{2}$" seam allowance. Press the seam allowance open.

2. Layer quilt top, batting, and pieced backing.

3. Quilt as desired. The Starscape quilt was stitched using a stylized leaf pattern over the entire quilt top.

4. Bind with brown-and-black print binding strips.

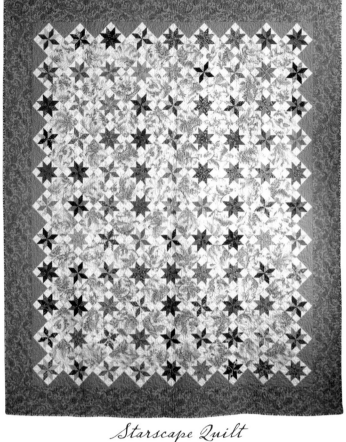

Starscape Quilt

Designed and pieced by Edyta Sitar;
machine quilted by Pam Henrys

Quilt Center Assembly Diagram

Quilt Top Assembly Diagram

Lily Dreams Table Runner

Materials

- 14" square light beige-grey batik for appliqué foundation
- 8–9" x 22" pieces (fat eighths) of assorted light prints and batiks for hourglass blocks
- 8–9" x 22" pieces (fat eighths) of assorted dark prints and batiks for hourglass blocks
- ⅛ yard multi-color batik for border
- ¼ yard green batik for binding
- 3–5" squares of assorted purple batiks for flower appliqués
- 6" x 8" rectangle gold batik for flower base and stem appliqués
- 6" x 8" rectangle brown print for vine appliqués
- 5" square of green batik for leaf appliqués
- 2 assorted orange print scraps for leaf appliqués
- 24" x 37" backing fabric
- 24" x 37" batting

Finished blocks: appliqué, 11½" square; hourglass, 2⅞" square

Finished table runner: 31" x 17¾"

Quantities are for 44/45"-wide, 100% cotton fabrics. Measurements include ¼" seam allowances. Sew with right sides together unless otherwise stated.

Cut the Fabrics

Note: Cut the hourglass and border pieces first. Use the leftover fabric for the appliqués.

From assorted light prints and batiks, cut:

16–4⅛" squares, cutting each diagonally in an X for a total of 64 triangles.

From assorted dark prints and batiks, cut:

16–4⅛" squares, cutting each diagonally in an X for a total of 64 triangles.

From multi-color batik, cut:

2–4¼" x 17¾" border strips

From green batik, cut:

3–2½" x 42" binding strips

Cut and Assemble the Appliqué Block

1. Use the appliqué method of your choice from pages 18–31 and the patterns on pages 66–67 to prepare the appliqué pieces.

From purple batiks, cut:

4 *each* of patterns B, C, and D

From gold batik, cut:

4 *each* of patterns A and I

From brown print, cut:

4 of pattern E

From green batik, cut:

4 *each* of patterns F and G

From orange print scraps, cut:

4 of pattern H

2. Position the appliqué pieces on the 14" light beige-grey batik foundation square. Appliqué the shapes in place using your favorite method. Press appliquéd block from the back. Center and trim it to 12" square.

Lily Dreams Table Runner

Assemble the Table Runner

1. Lay out two assorted light triangles and two assorted dark triangles. Sew together the triangles in pairs. Press seams toward darker triangles. Join pairs to make an hourglass block measuring $3\frac{3}{8}$" square. Press seams in one direction. Repeat to make 32 hourglass blocks.

Make 32

2. Sew together two rows of four hourglass blocks as shown. Press seams toward dark triangles. The horizontal rows should measure $3\frac{3}{8}$" x 12".

3. Join the rows to the appliqué block to make the center section of the table runner.

4. Sew together the remaining hourglass blocks in four rows of six blocks, referring to the diagram. Press seams toward dark triangles.

5. Sew the rows together in pairs; press seam allowances open.

6. Add pairs to long edges of center section. Press seams toward center section.

7. Sew $4\frac{1}{4}$" x $17\frac{3}{4}$" multi-color border strips to short edges of the table runner center. Press seams toward borders.

Complete the Table Runner

1. Layer table runner top, batting, and backing.

2. Quilt as desired. The table runner was quilted using neutral thread, stitched closely around the appliqué shapes and echo-quilted $\frac{1}{4}$" and $\frac{1}{2}$" beyond the shapes. The background and hourglass blocks are filled with an all-over floral pattern and a vine motif in the border.

3. Bind with green batik binding strips.

Lily Dreams Table Runner

Designed and pieced by Edyta Sitar; machine quilted by Julie Lillo

Rose Hip Heart Wallhanging

Materials

- 13½" square cream-and-pink print for appliqué foundation
- ⅜ yard green-brown batik for small triangles
- ⅜ yard multi-color pattern batik for large triangles
- ¾ yard green-brown pattern batik for border
- ¼ yard burgundy batik for corner squares
- ⅓ yard dark blue-green batik for binding
- 8" square dark brown print for stem appliqués
- 4 assorted green print and batik scraps for leaf appliqués
- 3 assorted red print and batik scraps for flower appliqués
- 3 assorted gold print and batik scraps for leaf and flower center appliqués
- Blue batik scrap for flower appliqués
- 39" square backing fabric
- 39" square batting

Finished appliqué block: 11" square
Finished wallhanging: 33" square

Quantities are for 44/45" wide, 100% cotton fabrics. Measurements include ¼" seam allowances. Sew with right sides together unless otherwise stated.

Cut the Fabric

Cut the corner square pieces first. Use leftover fabric for the flower appliqués.

From green-brown batik, cut:
1—12¼" square, cutting each diagonally in an X for a total of 4 small triangles.

From multi-color pattern batik, cut:
2—11⅞" squares, cutting each in half diagonally for a total of 4 large triangles.

From green-brown pattern batik, cut:
4—5¾" x 22½" border strips

From burgundy batik, cut:
4—5¾" corner squares

From dark blue-green batik, cut:
4—2½" x 42" binding strips

Cut and Assemble the Appliqué Block

1. Use the appliqué method of your choice from pages 18-31 and the patterns on pages 38-39 to prepare the appliqué pieces.

From dark brown print, cut:
1 *each* of patterns A, B, E, F, S, and T
2 *each* of patterns C and D

From green prints and batik scraps, cut:
1 *each* of patterns G, N, O, Q, U, and V
4 of pattern J
3 *each* of patterns L and M

From assorted red prints and batik scraps, cut:
6 of pattern H
1 of pattern P
2 of pattern R

From gold prints and batik scraps, cut:
6 of pattern I
2 of pattern L

From blue batik scraps, cut:
2 of pattern K

2. Position the appliqué pieces on 13½" cream-and-pink print foundation square. Appliqué the shapes in place using your favorite method. Press appliquéd block from the back. Center and trim to 11½" square.

Rose Hip Heart Wallhanging

Assemble the Wallhanging

1. Sew small green-brown batik triangles to opposite edges of the appliquéd block. Press seams toward the triangles. Add small triangles to remaining edges of appliquéd block. Press as before. The wallhanging center should be 16" square.

2. Sew large multi-color pattern triangles to opposite edges of the center. Press seams toward large triangles. Add large triangles to the remaining edges of the wallhanging. Press seams toward large triangles. The wallhanging center should be 22½" square.

3. Referring to Wallhanging Assembly Diagram, sew 5¾" x 22½" green-brown pattern border strips to opposite edges of wallhanging center. Press seams toward the border.

4. Add 5¾" burgundy squares to ends of each remaining border strip. Press seams toward border strip. Sew pieced borders to remaining edges of the wallhanging center. Press seams toward the border.

Complete the Wallhanging

1. Layer wallhanging top, batting, and backing.

Wallhanging Assembly Diagram

2. Quilt as desired. The wallhanging was stitched in-the-ditch of every seam and ¼" inside the first stitching on the block. To add dimension to the appliquéd block, it was machine-stitched around all the appliqués and echo-quilted to fill the background. A ¾" grid was stitched in the small triangles, a 1" grid in the border strips, and a heart design in the large triangles.

3. Bind with dark blue-green batik binding strips.

Rose Hip Heart Wallhanging

Designed and pieced by Edyta Sitar; machine quilted by Julie Lillo

Pincushions

Wondering what to do with those small treasures you've collected over the years, like old silver dishes, cupcake tins, antique trinkets, or even bottle lids from small jars? Pincushions are the perfect way to recycle those special things you can't part with into a treasure for family and friends.

Press your fabric. Use circle patterns slightly larger than the opening of your containers to trace circles on a variety of colors and fabric. Cut out the fabric circles.

Supplies—Assorted fabrics, circle patterns, variety of circular bases, tins, hot glue gun, strong cotton or DMC thread, sewing needle, and batting

Using a basting stitch, sew approximately $\frac{1}{4}$" around the edge of the circle .

Pull the stitches together to gather the edges of the fabric circle.

Stuff the gathered fabric circle with batting.

Here's a Tip
Pincushions are a perfect small gift for everyone to keep their pins organized. Now you're ready to make one using recycled treasures that are fun and important to share with friends and family. Add your own special flare!

Pull both ends of the gathering stitch together and tighten. Tie the threads together to make the pincushion.

Using the hot glue gun, place glue around the edges of the cup or dish being used as a base.

Place the pincushion on the base. Allow time for the hot glue to dry.

Circle pattern

Note: *This template is for the smallest pincushion (bottle cap), for larger sized bases add 2" to the diameter of the opening to determine the correct size.*

Finishing with a Label

It is a magnificent day when you add a special label to mark the end of a project that has taken countless hours. I love using appliquéd designs to create my own unique labels. Create labels with a block design inspired by your finished project or switch it up and commemorate the day with your own one-of-a-kind design.

Supplies—Traced block design, light fabric (batiks work wonderfully), a light box, and fabric pen.

Note: The Garden Grace block pattern on page 74 was used to create the label on this page.

1 Cut the fabric large enough to make the desired block size. Leave enough space to write your name, date, and any other special design elements you want to add. Place the traced block design and the fabric square right side up on the illuminated light box. Trace only the outside lines onto the fabric square. Do not trace the dotted lines.

2 After you have finished tracing the block design onto the fabric, add personal touches to the drawing. Emphasize parts of the block with shading, dots, or your own unique design style.

3 Add the date to the block and sign it. Attach the block to the back of the project with a small whipstitch.

Meet designer, Edyta Sitar . . .

Edyta's love for fabric began at a very young age - when she used her mother's newly hung drapes to create her first fabric project! Fortunately for all of us, her mother recognized her passion for fabric and thus began her journey with fabric and sewing.

Creating beautiful gowns ushered Edyta into creative textile design and established the building blocks which led her into a quilting adventure.

One of Edyta's biggest blessings is her marriage to husband, Michael. She not only fell in love, she was introduced to the family tradition of quilting by her mother-in-law, Carol, and grandmother-in-law, Anna.

With more than 64 years of quilting experience to share, Grandma Anna taught Edyta the basics of hand quilting and scrap piecing.

Mom and me

Anna Sitar

Her first sewing machine was a wedding gift from her mother-in-law, Carol. Edyta still has it and her daughters, Anna and Delfina, love to use it. "Mom (Carol) is my biggest fan, always cheering me on, encouraging me to stretch beyond my limits and take on any project."

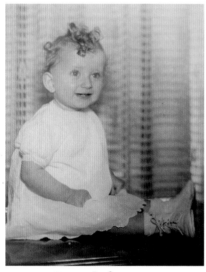

Carol Sitar

To an extent, quilting has opened a door to another world for Edyta, one in which she can express herself, create beautiful designs, and release her artistic passion. The combination of inspiration from nature, a love for fabric, a keen eye for color, and her family teachings blended into the recipe for developing a flourishing talent for designing quilts, fabrics, and quilting patterns.

"My children and my husband are my greatest motivation, providing the basis that you can accomplish anything you want if you just set your mind to it. Being able to do what I love and share this love with others is the greatest feeling and reward I could imagine! This is the Cinderella dream for me."

Her true love for quilting and her quilter's spirit shines through in her classes, workshops, and presentations. She travels all over sharing her passion, connecting to and inspiring quilters of all levels by sharing personal and stimulating stories about the quilts she makes.

As the owner and co-founder of Laundry Basket Quilts, her work has been published in magazines world-wide and her quilts have received numerous awards.

Edyta is proud to carry on a family tradition that fabrics and threads have seamlessly stitched together through the generations.

Edyta resides in Marshall, Michigan with her husband and children where she enjoys creating beautiful patterns for Laundry Basket Quilts and designing splendid fabrics for MODA.

Resources

Laundry Basket Quilts
www.laundrybasketquilts.com

Moda Fabrics
www.unitednotions.com

Julie Lillo - long arm quilter
www.quiltedjewels.com

Pam Henrys - long arm quilter
www.everlastingstitches.com

Craft Photographic Gallery
www.craftphotography.com

Southern Exposure
www.southernmoon.com

Landauer Corporation
www.landauercorp.com

Edyta's grandparents with their children

"Thank you Daddy"